After Words

Poetry by Joyce Sutphen

Straight Out of View (1995)

Coming Back to the Body (2000)

Naming the Stars (2004)

Fourteen Sonnets (2005)

First Words (2010)

House of Possibility (2012)

Joyce Sutphen

After Words

POEMS

Red Dragonfly Press ❧ Minnesota ❧ 2013

ISBN 978-1-937693-28-2
978-1-937693-29-9 (e-book)

Library of Congress Control Number: 2013932999

First Printing

Special thanks to Connie Wanek and Phil Dentinger — most of all for their friendship, but also for their steady encouragement as well as insightful and careful comments on the manuscript in progress. Thanks also to poets I admire (too many to list here) for inspiring me to keep making these "verbal contraptions," and thanks especially to Tim Nolan, Connie Wanek, Patricia Kirkpatrick, Phil Bryant, Phebe Hanson, John Rezmerski, Sharon Chmielarz, and Becky Fremo for sharing their new work and listening to mine. I am grateful for residencies at the Anderson Center in Minnesota and Fundación Valparaiso in Almeria, Spain where some of these poems were written, and also to my colleagues at Gustavus Adolphus College for encouragement and support that made new work possible during an extraordinarily busy time. Thanks to my family for inspiring me to consider and remember. Thanks for being there Walt. Finally, many thanks to Scott King at Red Dragonfly Press for encouragement over the years and for making another beautiful book.

Due to space limitations publication acknowledgments are printed at the back of this book.

Cover image: photograph by Joyce Sutphen

Typeset in Minion, a digital type designed by Robert Slimbach

Printed in the United States of America
on 30% recycled stock
by BookMobile, a 100% wind powered company

Published by Red Dragonfly Press
press-in-residence at the Anderson Center
P. O. Box 406
Red Wing, MN 55066

For more information and additional titles visit our website
www.reddragonflypress.org

Contents

For all of my family—parents, children, grandchildren, brothers and sisters, aunts and uncles, cousins, nieces and nephews, in-laws and out-laws too.

A Dream of Empty Fields

As I read your words, I'm thinking along
with you, remembering a place I loved
the way you loved the place you are telling
me about. I know just what you mean here.

And when you say how it felt when you lost
that ground, how it was covered with cement
and brick and steel, I say I know how that
feels; I see houses where there once were fields,

street signs on corners that were open land,
stop signs to halt the traffic that began
as soon as they put a road through the field—
gas stations, grocery stores, everything.

Just once, I'd like to see them take it down,
pack up the houses, put away the town.

In Winter

In winter, snow drifted in through a crack
in the hay-barn door. Up there it was cold,
and the stacks of bales looked like cliffs of green
that we climbed so we could throw the hay down

to the chute and into the barn where it was warm.
Down in the barn, the heads of the cows turned
towards us when we broke open the bales and
forked chunks of alfalfa into their cribs.

We were in the middle of Bethlehem,
and "Away in a Manger" was always
playing while the kind eyes of Holsteins gazed
on us with all the love we'd ever need.

Later, walking across the yard, we saw
the brightest star over the hay-barn roof.

Those Kids

We walked on top of the snow, our bodies
so light we seldom broke through, although
we expected to and held our arms out
like wings.

It would be a long time before we could
go in, we knew that. Peace must reign at least
an hour; she must be able to hear clocks
ticking,

the tea pot whistling, the quiet voices
in the radio. The waxed floor must dry
and then we would be allowed back again —
but not

before that. If we got cold, there was always
the barn, where the cows stood in their stanchions,
each one throwing off heat like a furnace,
the steam

coming out of their nostrils as they chewed
the hay we stored above them in the loft,
watching over us as the
night fell.

Kris Kringles at the Farm

The object was not to give
but to be as secretive
as the red fox in the gravel pit.

You were one of nine (to narrow
it down a bit) — none of whom
had anything but a name

on a piece of paper drawn
from the hat — and that
was the object:

to figure out who had whom
or who knew who did
and keep it secret

as a scrap of paper
swallowed as they
closed in on you.

Things I Liked About Christmas

I liked those scrawny trees
that leaned to one side, and you
always had to add a branch
to the open spot in the middle,

and I liked those colored bulbs
exploding with a flash and a pop,
and the ones like lava lamps
that could never settle on a branch,

and there was nothing under the tree
except the little town of Bethlehem—
looking more like Pennsylvania
than Palestine in the snowy hills,

and then, on Christmas morning,
the presents—unwrapped and
mostly practical, but always
that one special thing—

a blue typewriter for me,
BB guns for my brothers,
a Chatty Cathy for my little sister,
and a pedal tractor for the baby.

You were always the best gift—
watching through the French doors
from the kitchen, making sure
everything came out even.

Making Gingerbread Cookies

I could tell you how good they smelled:
(cloves and ginger mixed with molasses)
and I could tell you how the dough
flattened out under the rolling pin
and the way the cookie cutter stamped
out an army of gingerbread people.

You should imagine later—
the bodies piled on one end of the table
and all of us at work, quickly
spreading the skin of frosting
from head to toe and then adding
the eyes, the nose, and the smile.

Dairyland

Long before I ever heard of Disneyland,
I went to Dairyland with my father,
where he lifted the silver cans of milk
out of his pick-up truck and sent them
down the rollers to the dairy men,
in their white coats and white hats,
waiting to empty each can and send it
through the washer and back out, clanging
like a bell in the church of milk and cream.

I waited in the truck, reading *The Black*
Stallion and *Trixie Belden*. It was
Christmas vacation and cold. Steam drifted
out from the dairy and settled in the trees.
When I looked up, the world was as white as milk.

Everyday Disasters

The tidal wave of milk
across the kitchen table—

"Every meal," my mother
said. "It's always something,"

said my father, watching
the storm clouds overhead.

Just then my brother came
running in, his head all

bloody from a Lawn Jart
that went astray, and that

was the same day he was
bitten by a squirrel

and nearly drowned.
The rest of us never cried

except for every
little thing—a faulty

reed, a key that stuck,
the slightest criticism.

Still, it's all the same to us—
We don't expect much.

The trains roar through the marsh;
the stars slip through the branches—

everyday disasters,
just waiting to happen.

The Family

We were never meant to stay together,
but each of us had something that matched us
to the rest — the way we held a stranger's
gaze, how we could stand at the edge of talk

and never say a word. We all had that
same smile and the same ability to
disappear without warning. We knew our
way around the fields and woods; we knew how

to build a shelter out of sticks and leaves,
how to clear a yard and stock a pantry.
The only thing we feared was the fox who
prowled the gravel pit and the circling hawk.

We never saw a shadow in the leaves,
the small death that ended every day.

The Family Dreams

When my brother dreams, he can swim
through air, just above the ground
in a park near the lake. Easy
he says.

And in my daughter's dream, there are a dozen
puppies, replicas of the brilliant Luna, who
could cook an omelet
or mail a letter.

My father dreams of haystacks and bringing
milk to the dairy. He sees people who
left the planet a half-century ago.
He ascends.

My mother wakes often and when she sleeps she dreams
of numbers marching through the kitchen — 3,000
washdays, 22,000 suppers, and a single diamond.
She finds herself awake again.

Me? I rarely dream. It's a curse I brought on myself
when I said that I didn't want to talk about
my dreams, that I didn't believe in
the power of suggestion.

Uncle Al in the Early 60's

At the kitchen table he's teaching us
Buck Euchre and letting us win a hand

or two. It's a game I never play
again, but for a moment in 1961

I understand it perfectly. Next morning,
he lets us keep Dion on the car radio:

"I'm the kind of guy who likes to roam around
. . . I roam around and round and round and round."

In the cafe, he buys us glazed donuts
and gives us quarters for the jukebox.

We play "Runaround Sue," "Wolverton
Mountain," and (of course) "The Wanderer,"

while he sits at the counter drinking coffee,
smiling at our reflections in the mirror.

Uncle Al and Uncle Floyd Shoot Some Pool

They're wearing white shirts
and their flowered ties hang
on the brass doorknob.

Uncle Floyd rubs the tip
of his cue with a square
of blue chalk, and Uncle Al

leans over the table to take
a shot, teeth clenched down
on his cigar. I'm as tall as

the pool table, and I can see
the green felt cloth and the
rolling balls, solid and striped.

Uncle Al wipes the sweat from
his forehead, says: "Now that's
a real trick shot!" Uncle Floyd

sways to one side, makes
the floor creak. I'm so close
I can see his fingernails are etched

with fine lines, that the cue's blue
nudge is slipping back and forth
on the bony rack of his fingers.

There's something tightening,
gathering itself to strike.
Bam! I see that he has divided

the triangle of Heaven so that
each bright planet will find
a deep pocket and sleep
until the green sky is empty.

Say Uncle

In the Fifties, my uncles wore felt hats
and smoked Dutch Masters. They drove
black cars trimmed with silver chrome, those cars that
when you see them now in films, make you love

the past more than you ever thought you would.
They were young, jackets slung
over their shoulders, all of them good
husbands, fathers — not a mean one among

them. They were like plain-clothed angels, our own
squadron keeping the lawns free
of goblins and bears, rolling the huge stone
from the mouth of the cave so that we could see

that there wasn't anything to be done:
night would always come — and then the sun.

The Bones of Horses

They buried horses, didn't they? And their bones
turned up years later in the graves of trees
overturned, uprooted like dark backbones,
wind ripping across the level prairies.

The rain came down in wide sheets, gathering
in the ditches, or making a blue eye
of an empty socket in the road. Rings
when you find them are magic; why

wonder where the horses went, or wish
them back again? Just think: they kept us close
together; they were not made of wire mesh
and steel riding strips of tar. We chose

for ease and power, for the thrill of speed;
we buried what we thought we didn't need.

Old Machinery

On the edge of the woods
or in the weeds behind the shop
were things gone useless —

horse-drawn mower,
long-toothed side-rake,
hay-loader, tall as a giraffe —

gathered together as if
to testify to a past that was
as wide as a team of horses.

The White-Washed Barn

Chalky-white, dove-grey over the clean-scrubbed
barn walls, ceilings swept clear of cobwebs, the
swallow's nests knocked down into the gutters.

The brush-tip of broomstick dipped in the pail,
the lift and swish of the bristles, soft, like
milk, drying to a thickness that would chip,

flake, lift off in puzzle pieces one night
in winter when the cows stood mindful calm
in the white-walled barn, the yellow straw

spread beneath them, the rust-green of silage
mounded in the stone cribs on either side
of the aisle, where we played, aware of
the lives of animals, the snows, drifting.

Taking Stock

I

Even when you couldn't see him
you knew he was standing
in the open door of the hay barn,
covered with a fine white powder of dust,
lifting gunnysacks of oats,
shoveling the dried ears of corn
into the wide throat of the hammer-mill.

Later, in the barn below the hay barn,
he'd slide open the ground-feed chute,
let pour a gold dusty stream into
the basket propped on his knee,
then bump the tin bushel along
top of the cement crib, measuring
each portion with a scoop, according to
some arcane calculation in pounds of milk
and butterfat. "It's like dessert to them,"
he said, meaning the cows.

II

He's always been a good dreamer,
the kind who could dream about the stars
bowing down to the earth or seven
fat cows devoured by seven lean cows.
He'd tell his dream
to anyone who wanted to hear it.
All week, after it happened,
he had the same dream:
he was smoothing a piece of wood,
sanding it down and seeing the grain,
clear as gravel washed in a stream,
so real, he said, you wanted to touch it,
rub your hand along its soft side.

III

If I try to hold him still,
I never can.
He's down in the meadow

cutting hay
and when he sees me waving,
he waves back,
big circles over his head, one arm
dancing free . . .
Mr. Bojangles.

Or he is hurrying from
one milk machine to another,
checking, adjusting, timing it
so that one by one,
he can finish milking each cow,
pull the vacuum hose from
the nozzle, unhook the milker
(and the long leather belt
that holds the milker in place),
step out from between cows,
hold the belt and hose up high
to balance
the steaming weight of the milker
as he walks to the milk can
and pours a white-fall of fresh milk
into the stainless-steel strainer,
pauses, and then turns
to hook the empty milker
to another cow,
adjusting the belt, and then
leaps up to the next milker
(almost filled now) or pauses
to make an adjustment on
the one in-between or the one
jangled by a cow who kicks
and tries to dance the milker
into the wall . . .

IV

Or I see him
getting onto his "H" tractor—
the way a cowboy in the old Westerns
mounts his horse—
and talking, waving, as he swings a leg

over the seat, settling his hands
on the wheel and throttle,
letting out the clutch
and galloping off.

Or maybe he's pulling away
with a wagon piled high with hay,
jumping down to open the gate,
leaping back up to drive through,
jumping down to close the gate,
leaping back to drive up the hill
to the wooden feeders he made last fall,
stopping at each one, lifting,
breaking open the bales with a thrust of his knee,
pulling back on the twine to spill
the chunks of hay into the feeder.

And sometimes he's at the gas pump,
as if he's brought his horse to water,
or sometimes he is arc welding in the shop,
menacing in his black welding mask,
until he stops for a minute, pushes up
the mask to say "Look away now,"
and other times he's spraying apple
blossoms in Spring or digging potatoes
in Fall, or pruning the grapevines
or piling wood in long piles, like cars
on a freight train that goes rolling by.
And sometimes he is sitting at the table,
the newspaper spread out in front of him,
coffee cup steaming at his elbow
and a minute later he's leaned back
in the chair, sleeping. . . .

V

It takes a long time, but finally
I begin asking the right questions
and I ask them more than once
until I know the answers by heart.

Making Hay at Jimmy Willikee's

Because I loved the sound of his name,
and because his land was hilly (and ours
wasn't) and his place was on the other

side of town, I always wanted to help
with making hay at Jimmy Willikee's.

It was like going to the moon, somewhere
foreign, where cows had horns and church bells
rang unexpectedly over the trees.
At noon, we stopped to eat our sandwiches
and drink cold water from a mason jar—
the ice just little floating flecks of white.

I wondered why Jimmy Willikee let
us cut his hay—wasn't hay the best thing
in the world? He must be a very rich man
(that Jimmy Willikee) to have so much
hay that he could let us come and make
it into bales that we would drive slowly

along the almost impossible road
between Jimmy Willikee's place and ours.

The Scythe

The scythe escaped the fire that burned the plow
and the oat-binder, that burned the baler
and the side-rake, burned the cultivator,
the field-chopper, the harrow, and the disk.

It was not hanging from a wall with the
hammers and the pliers; it was not on
the workbench with the anvil and the vice;
it wasn't on the hook above the door

or leaning against a wall with
the rake, the shovel, the sledge-hammer, or
the broom; no, the scythe was whispering to
itself, hidden in the long grass

where the mower let it drop, distracted
by something sweeter than fact or fire.

The Come Back

He was eighty-seven, and one day he
made a wrong step on an icy sidewalk

and he fell, breaking his hip. It was just
past dawn, and he'd gone out to put some wood

in the furnace that heated the house. Down
on his hands and knees, he crawled across

the yard but couldn't climb the steps or yell
loud enough to wake the sleepers sleeping

in their warm rooms, so he pounded against
the side of the house, and they found him there.

After that, it was just a matter of repair,
repair. The ice melted; the days grew warm

and green. He learned to walk again, to lift
each foot as in a dance — each step a gift.

Apple Trees at the Farm

Like the people they
have grown ancient.

Props assist the branches,
the trunks are cracked

and yellow leaves (a few)
are on the boughs

even in July. I do not
want these trees to die.

Look — the old trees
are heavy with apples.

Surely those who
carry such weight

will be here forever.

Our Fathers

Our fathers, who lived all their lives on earth —
are going now. They have given us all
we need, and when we asked, they gave us more.

Their names are beautiful to us, holy
as the names of stars, as familiar
as the roads we traveled, falling asleep

on the way from one farm to another.
Their kingdoms were small; they were never
interested in more than one homestead,

and as for evil: although they could not
keep it from us, they tried to keep us from
temptation, though we were like all children

and wanted our own power and glory,
world without end, forever and amen.

News of the World

My mother and my best friend both
email me to say it's a good day
for hanging wash.

Right then, Love called me to some things:
dish towels, white t-shirts, my daughter's
pajamas.

Just before noon all the William Morris
sheets and pillowcases were filled
with the spring wind.

I don't know what sort of balance I should
keep — delicate or difficult?
Either one. Both.

"Perfect Weather for Hanging Wash"

The church bell rings one time.
It could be one o'clock
or half past any hour.
How quickly I can do nothing.

At dinner we fill each other's
glasses with wine and spoon the soup
into each bowl. Someone makes a fire,
someone slices bread. We all talk.

Walking down to the beach today —
the blue Mediterranean
behind the white houses, I thought
of my mother — what she would say.

My Mother's Secret Life

At the table or leaning on the counter,
sometimes — if there was a lull or a little
space between the afternoon and starting
supper, we could get my mother to draw

horses, and every horse was perfect:
fine head and arched neck, the ears pitched forward
inquisitively, shoulders and back sloped
and shadowed with a curve, and then the legs —

long and shapely, tapered to the ankle
and hooves: running, galloping, standing still,
a horse we would want to keep, a prototype
of all the ones we'd meet in books, later.

As for the guitar up in the attic,
we never asked what she could do with that.

The Exam

It is mid-October. The trees are in
their autumnal glory (red, yellow-green,

orange) outside the classroom where students
take the mid-term, sniffling softly as if

identifying lines from Blake or Keats
was such sweet sorrow, summoned up in words

they never saw before. I am thinking
of my parents, of the six decades they've

been together, of the thirty thousand
meals they've eaten in the kitchen, of the

more than twenty thousand nights they've slept
under the same roof. I am wondering

who could have fashioned the test that would have
predicted this success? Who could have known?

Ironing Board

It folded out of the wall
the way a person opens her mouth to say

"ah." Standing straight as
a soldier in a guard house,

it came down flat, a runway
for the heavy black iron

that had burned its face
into the ironing board cover.

My Mother at the Sewing Machine

It was a Singer, with an iron
treadle and a silver foot
that lifted up and down.

She kept it in her closet
in front of the window — pins and
needles sticking in the curtains.

Sewing, she could see us
playing in the sandpile,
making roads and pie tin lakes,

and across the garden — past
the road going up the hill —
my father cultivating corn.

Every seam she stitched
seemed straight enough
to hold us all together.

Elemental [The Golden Book of Dreams]

My mother is a fish. No. Someone else,
in a story, made that mistake, but I

mean it differently, as in: My mother
is a rabbit at the edge of the lawn,

warning me to stay out of the toolshed,
but I am distracted and will, of course, go

where I should not go, and so later,
in a chamomile haze, I think my mother

is a horse in the golden book that she
reads to me each night when I am four,

and I am the pony with the long legs,
following a road that winds up and down

the valleys until I am lost and then
my mother is a white owl gliding from

one tree to another, ahead of me,
above me, silently leading me home.

The Old-Fashioned Future

In that future, which is now
already past, all of us flew
our own little spaceships

and wore shiny jumpsuits
of silver and blue. Robots
made our breakfast (the usual

glass of instant something) and
served it to us in our chrome
and glass kitchens while

the bed made itself and a
newspaper scrolled out
of the wall. There were dog

robots chasing cat robots
and buildings like mixers
and blenders spiking up

in the pink Martian sky.
We played golf on the moon
and everyone spoke

the language of the stars.
In that old future, the horizons
were quiet, and the only

thing we worried about was
when to press that single
computer button at the

sprockets factory and
whether or not we should
move to Jupiter in the Spring.

Danger Days

Back in the old danger days,
when we were kids, we stood
on the front seat of the Chevy Impala —
no seat belts to hold us back,
our mother's arm the only thing
between us and the dashboard,

though sometimes they strapped us
into contraptions hooked over
the back of the seat, our chubby legs
dangling down, our small hands
gripping the frame — all set to be
launched through the windshield!

And it is one of the wonders of
American life that most of us
survived to drive those cars to the
outdoor movies so we could watch
Easy Rider while the crop-dusting planes
passed low overhead and the mosquito

control-trucks sprayed DDT down
the streets of our town, a trail of kids
on bicycles following behind. And it
probably never occurred to us what
a Lawn Jart could do — we were too busy
worrying about the end of the world.

Grandma Clara

About noon she arrived in her blue and
white Bel Air by Chevrolet, in which she
did not see the USA but only

the road from her house in town to the farm
she built with her husband, who died as soon
as they retired, and that is why she came

each day — just to have something to do, to
help us with the work we had inherited
from her: the strawberry fields, gardens,

apple orchards and grapevines, rhubarb stalks,
potato patch, rows of sweet corn, wild plums,
and gooseberries — and all those fields of corn

and oats and hay, pastures too, above the
house and woods or down by the meadow where
the green grass grew. Who would not return to

such a place? I see her walking across
the lawn in her straw hat, hoe in hand,
ready to chop away whatever weeds

dared grow between the perfectly mounded
hills of potatoes, those rows that would feed
us all through the cold white winter when she

would come less often though we would see her
every morning in the back of church —
praying, no doubt, for the whole crop of us.

That Woman, My Grandmother

That woman, my grandmother,
who could shock oats faster than a man,
is gone now.

Sometimes I think I see her
walking the fields,
a bundle under each arm —

until she reaches the place
where one thing
must lean against another —

she sets the bundles head to head,
two by two,
like lovers who know

they only have the night
before
the terrible threshing begins.

Overnight

There was a fluorescent rosary
on the bed stand and a clock
with numbers that glowed.

All night the lights from passing cars
would cut through the venetian blinds
reflecting across the walls,

so I would count cars in the dark
(but never the beads) wondering
if there was a meaning there.

September Afternoon, Writing

In my grandmother's time,
the afternoon was filled
with apples — apple peelings, apple
cores, apple pies, and applesauce.

In the afternoons, there were
grapes turning purple on the vines
at the garden's edge, pumpkins
ripening in the last warm days.

I came walking home from school,
carrying an empty lunch box
and a bag of homework.
I can't remember any of that.

My grandmother would have
wondered what I am doing here —
without a decent paring knife,
and these pages filled with scribbling.

My Grandmother Sells Her Strawberry Field

That would have been the year my brother Rick
was born, the year my brother Kevin turned

one; my sister Nancy was about three;
my brother Dan was four (or five — it all

depends on when it happened). I was
eleven; my sister Betty was nine

(or ten), and my brothers Mike and Joe were
eight and seven (close enough). We were all

so young! My parents were thirty-something,
and though my grandmother was sixty-three,

she'd been a widow for almost ten years.
That would have been the year she decided

that a strawberry field doesn't have to
last forever and love is all there is.

The Queen of Summer Lawns

Someone must be queen of the afternoon.
Someone must sit at the top of the steps
with a dark pink hollyhock in her hair.

We must call her "Your Majesty"
and scatter roses and petunia
petals on the steps before her. She must

wear a dandelion bracelet and a
crown of grape leaves. She must sit very still.
When she is thirsty, we will give her red

nectar to drink; when she is hungry, we
will feed her vegetables from the garden.
We will guard her kingdom from the gravel

road to the apple trees. No stranger shall
approach her: winter winds will stay away
forever, and the snows will never come.

Boxes

I've opened the box from my mother's attic,
the one she made me take home because
although she doesn't want to keep anything,

there are some things she can't throw away,
like these old papers and notebooks from the last
days of Camelot, when JFK was president

and my sister stayed home with rheumatic fever.
I bring the box home, but I don't look at it
for almost a year, and then one day, I do.

I open it up and lift things out onto the table —
a project called "My Book of Uganda," with a map
that the teacher says "could be colored" but is "nice and neat"

and a missionary story that my sister certainly
did not write. I prefer the next project, which
is called "Our Clothes," and I especially like

"Ways We Care for Our Clothing": "Wear
aprons," "Put them in our drawers," "Don't tear
our clothes," and "Wear them nice on our bodies."

And I remember that she grew up just
enough — at sixteen — to wear her clothes
very nicely on her body, and I thank the sheep

that she mentions in her book — the ones that
gave their wool for our clothes, and the men
who took care of the sheep and also my

mother, who my sister thanks for making her
clothes, and who made the green dress that she
wore into the grave and into the forever after.

Cover

It's the front of a heavy folder,
meant to gather loose school papers,

or it's a brown envelope large enough
for a child's dress and socks, folded flat

and filed away when no longer of use,
or it once held something — a book,

if the small black print next to the
Chicago address is to be trusted.

It occurs to me that everything I am
trying to tell you is in print, and that

I could copy it, line by line, as in:
first, the name of the school over

the name of the town and state (and you
would notice that this was before zip codes

and two-letter state abbreviations), then,
a long blank line and under it "Name of Pupil,"

then, down, down, in the middle of the page:
"A. J. Daniel Co." in typeface twice as large

as the next line: "Funeral Home." There's more,
of course: the address, and a phone number:

238 W. That's it — 238 W. How is that a phone
number? And what sort of school has a funeral

home furnish the children with folders? I would
like to know the answer to one of these questions.

My Sister's School Papers

Her handwriting is very different from mine.
I'm messier. I write larger and spell better
because I haven't been lying in bed for months,
lost in the heart's faltering chambers.

Most of the papers are arithmetic problems
and worksheets about stories they've read.
For example: "In the story, 'The Boy
with the Bass Drum,' Joey prays because
a) the parade was a success, b) he discovered
the horrors of war, c) he wanted his father to return
safely, or d) he was grateful not to be hungry."
"d" — My sister got that one right, and I can tell
she had read the story because if she hadn't,
she would have guessed "b" ("he discovered
the horrors of war").

It's a long worksheet in six parts,
and she misses only one question on the first page.
The "Vocabulary Section" and "Recalling Details"
are perfect, and she sorts the adverbs
from the verbs and the compound words (no problem),
but in the section that requires her to divide
each word into syllables and place the primary accent,
she gets every one of them wrong —
she loses 17 points on 15 words!
I realize she must have been missing the day
they learned about stress, too tired and pale
even to be carried up the steps to the classroom.

Later, I'll call my brother and tell him
that in the quiz about Paraguay, she got every
question right, including the capital (Asunción)
and the name of the native people (the Guaraní),
but — no surprise — she misspelled Jesuit.

Generally, she does well in Religion tests, but
her essays are very cautious. I know this because
I am in one and am much better behaved than I
ever was in real life. I like the way she ends
her essay about "What a Catholic Education
Means to Me": "When I am older," she says,
"my education will help me understand more things
in the world and help me get to Heaven."
I hope at least one of those things is true.

Two Girls on a Hay Rack

We're elbow to elbow,
hip to hip, my right arm to her
left, her left knee to my right.

Our feet are dangling down.
Someone has put us there
on the wagon, someone who

is holding the camera — a Brownie
Instamatic — who has stepped back
in order to get the entire rack

and its beautiful shadow
into the picture. It's afternoon
says the way the light falls;

it's hot says the ground.
"We're alive" say the girls,
"Click" goes the camera.

The Blue in the Distance

The blue in the distance is April,
and April is coming up the meadow,
crossing the river at the place where
the rocks line up like beads on a
string and we can walk across in
August—but not in April when the
waters are deep and move swiftly
under the slow skin warming in the sun.

The gold light falling into the blue
is the past, that other country where
the fields are undivided and houses
come with barns and silos and sheds
or go to live with other houses in
a place called town. That is how
the past was in the golden light.
Now there are houses everywhere.

The line on the horizon is very
thin and black. It draws the twig
on the branch and the branch on
the tree. It divides the ground
from the sky and follows the hill
up and down the valley—
whatever comes, whatever goes,
that line will carry it to your eye.

The green is the most surprising
thing of all. It comes up from
the ground, comes through
the branches in the air, comes
after the black, blue, and the gold.
The green grass, the green leaf,
the green dress that we wear
all summer long and into the grave.

Things I Know

I know how the cow's head turns
to gaze at the child in the hay aisle;

I know the way the straw shines
under the one bare light in the barn.

How a chicken pecks gravel into silt
and how the warm egg rests beneath

the feathers — I know that too, and
what to say, watching the rain slide

in silver chains over the machine
shed's roof. I know how one pail

of water calls to another and how
it sloshes and spills when I walk

from the milkhouse to the barn.
I know how the barn fills and

then empties, how I scatter lime
on the walk, how I sweep it up.

In the silo, I know the rung under
my foot; on the tractor, I know

the clutch and the throttle; I slip
through the fence and into the woods,

where I know everything: trunk
by branch by leaf into sky.

Fairy Tales

I think my favorite one
is about those children
(the boy and the girl — you know,
Hansel and Gretel) and how
their stepmother convinces
their father to take them into
the woods and leave them
for the wolves and the bears

and how they find their way back
with the help of white stones
that shine in the moonlight and
then how they are taken further
in and meet the witch (or is it
the stepmother in disguise?)
in the gingerbread house and
how she fattens them so that

she can eat them (greedy thing!)
and Gretel tricks her into climbing
into the oven and then "Ding
Dong, the Witch is Dead!" and
Hansel and Gretel fill their pockets
with diamonds and pearls and
ride across the water on a duck's
back to their father, who is living

alone now without the woman
who hated them so of course they
all live happily ever after. I like
this story because it's about a
failed attempt at murder, because it
expresses a fairly egalitarian relationship
between siblings and because it taught
me never to eat a wall or a window.

My First Kitchen

The stove is fiery red.
We lift the cast-iron lid
and push in a piece of wood.

When the oven opens, the door
screeches as if the wicked witch,
dead now (just blackened crust)

is moaning. The curtains
floating in the window above
the sink are green. A figure

crosses the lawn and opens
the door to the back porch. It is
my grandmother with the newspaper.

The Parish Grade School

The children sit in rows of
desks bolted to the floor.

When they lift the desktops
pencils slide, the hinges creak.

The teacher is a nun,
dressed like a nun from head

to toe; she wears a white
wimple and long black veil.

They go to mass each day
before school; the priest wears

purple vestments and swings
a thurible out and in. Incense

drifts over the first and second
grades. Back in the classroom,

the alphabet (in big and little)
frames the top of the chalkboard;

the numbers (in apples and ducks)
are arranged on the felt board.

At storytime, the children move
shyly to the front of the room

like birds to a feeder, like the
kittens lapping milk in the story.

Three Girls on Skates

I look down into the viewfinder's gray
blur — this was when you didn't get what you
saw; this was in the days of black and white.

My friends, standing in the schoolyard, have their
woolen scarves tied tightly under the chin;
they have snow pants pulled over their dresses,

and their woolen coats come down to the knee,
but it's because of the skates, polished white,
that I took the picture, using the box

camera that must have come from somewhere,
from those indulgent parents I never
knew, the same ones who flooded the garden

to make a place for us to skate. Who would
have thought life had ever been so good?

The One True Choir

First thing, she arranged us in rows
at the front of the classroom,
tallest in back, smallest in front.

Next, she pulled the shining pitch-
pipe from the hidden placket
in her black linen habit,

put it to her lips, then held it in front
of her, put it back to her lips and blew.
That day's note was like

a chain on the flagpole. We opened
our books and began to sing, "Faith
of our fathers, living still."

Her hands made sails and half-moons
in the air; her lips made the words stand
still so that we could step from note

to note, "in spite of dungeon, fire,
and sword," as the chorus rolled back
and forth over the morning sun.

Piano

Somehow, it keeps itself in tune.
Each key remembers its name
and loves its neighbors —
black and white.

No matter how many times I pass
without touching, it doesn't
refuse me when I finally lean over
and tell it where I've been.

My hands find the way slowly —
a few chords moving to
a hymn, a little ragtime,
and then the *Minuet in G.*

The hammers swing back
and hit the wires stretched between
the silver pegs — each note as long
as a pedal can hold it.

In the Wedding Pictures

You were so young then
and everyone else was
young then too—

except for the grandparents
and great aunts and uncles
we never knew.

Even your parents (our
grandparents) were young—
younger than I am now

as I write this from your
granddaughter's house as I
wait for my grandson

(your great-grandson)
to wake and eat his strawberries,
toast, and milk.

It's October. In the
wedding pictures, it's
1948, and you don't smile

until it's all over—but then you
smile brilliantly, surrounded by
your families, who must

already know how well you
will learn to do this—who must
imagine us, watching it happen.

With Child

I used to live somewhere
far away from now,

and if you dug a hole straight
through the planet

you would have found me
on the other side

bare-legged in my blue denim
dress, my shape smooth and round

in the middle where the baby
curled upside down, sucking

her thumb. I used to sit
in the sun, rubbing a clay pot

with a silver spoon, carving
stems and leaves, watching

the clouds come over the hills,
and I used to feel the baby's

feet pushing on my ribs
and the skin stretching to fit her

turning, though I thought
that nothing would ever happen,

that there was no such country
where I would be delivered.

Bell Bottom Baby

When she was one I cut
a pattern in blue denim

and sewed the pieces together.
Simplicity simple, elastic waistband.

The pants flared out into bells
with one-inch cuffs at the bottom,

but the part that amazes me is how
I sat for hours with an embroidery hoop,

stitching a Jacobean flower garden
to trail down each small leg,

knowing how quickly she'd
grow out of everything I did.

The Suzuki Mother

That was me, standing
behind the child,
adjusting the violin
on her shoulder,
straightening the wrist
so that it formed a perfect
angle, elbow to hand,
fingers placed squarely upon
the yellow lines
that crossed the fingerboard.

That was me, humming along
as I watched the music,
counting silently, hoping
each note into being,
more disciplined for her
than I'd ever been for myself
when I practiced piano in the sun porch,
skipping the hardest notes,
ignoring the fingerings —
all drama and flourish.

And that was me too,
thinking I had no expectations,
that I only wanted them
to find something they loved
and do it well —
when the truth was I wanted
an Itzhak Perlman
or a Yehudi Menuhin —
a little prodigy to call my own.

What That Was

I have forgotten so much. The day
I was born? I have forgotten that,

and I have forgotten sleeping
in the crib and waking up to wonder

what would happen next, and the day
I learned to walk — my first steps across

the kitchen floor — I can't remember that,
and my first word (what was it I said?)

and how it felt to be lifted up and
carried across the lawn, and learning to

put letters into words, words into
sentences, to disappear inside the page —

I have forgotten how I learned to do
that and how my body grew taller

and broke and bled and healed again;
I have forgotten learning I was not

a man and that I could carry another
person in my body and deliver her

into the world. I have forgotten so much —
except for that. I'll never forget that.

After That

I began with the last line of one poem,
which reminded him of the beginning

of another. And so these two poems —
one about lying in a hammock at a farm

in Minnesota, the other about
a legendary head we can never

know — will always come together in my
mind. When is it too late to revise your

life? How many lives does it take to fill
a hammock? And after you have seen the

butterfly sleeping on the trunk and the
chicken hawk floating over, it must be

your life is perfectly in tune, ready
for whatever it is comes after that.

We Have Come This Far

After you died, everything changed.
When I could no longer talk to you
I told myself things you said years

before. I thought of you as many
different people at once, old and young.

After you died, you could see into
the future and explain the past. Often
I would sit out in my chair on the lawn
and listen to you all afternoon. I asked
for advice, and yours was always good.

Of course it took some time before we
reached this happiness. I am aware
that you may have gone on to do other
things, that this world may no longer
concern you, but for me this is a way

to remember you. I suppose I don't
need to say that you are well now,
cured of that thing that killed you,
and planning to buy outrageous
hats and travel more frequently.

You're the only one I listen to
some days. Your sense of humor has
returned, and often we laugh all night.
As you may have noticed, I have been
adding color to everything, because

I know that pleases you. I hear you
telling me to love the things of this world—
the white pines, the sumac, flowers
in gardens and shells on the shore.
I see them with your eyes and say I do.

The Return

When I returned to the body this time
I was old; I had fallen
into my skin.

In the years when I was away
the sky filled and emptied itself
a thousand times

while I bent over the page
or sat in the assembly, my thoughts
in the bronze distance.

I had not learned how to love myself
when I was young, but I would
begin at last—

in my most unlovely age
I would send affection
along the nerve,

warmth to the smallest vein
and courage in the bone.

Next Time

I'll know the names of all of the birds
and flowers, and not only that, I'll
tell you the name of the piano player

I'm hearing right now on the kitchen
radio, but I won't be in the kitchen,

I'll be walking a street in
New York or London, about
to enter a coffee shop where people
are reading or working on their
laptops. They'll look up and smile.

Next time I won't waste my heart
on anger; I won't care about
being right. I'll be willing to be
wrong about everything and to
concentrate on giving myself away.

Next time, I'll rush up to people I love,
look into their eyes, and kiss them, quick.
I'll give everyone a poem I didn't write,
one specially chosen for that person.
They'll hold it up and see a new
world. We'll sing the morning in,

and I will keep in touch with friends,
writing long letters when I wake from
a dream where they appear on the
Orient Express. "Meet me in Istanbul,"
I'll say, and they will.

Dominoes

It's partly about dumb luck
and partly about getting rid of
things that will count against you
when someone goes out. Someone

goes out because they are lucky,
because they pay attention, and
because they put down the right
thing at the just the right time

and you don't. You know
that you will always lose this game,
but you play it anyway because
you love the little bone yard in

the middle of the table and how,
for a few moments after each game
you scc your own hands shuffling
the bones along with the familiar

hands of your mother and your father
who are telling stories that make you
forget to put down the double blank,
or to look over to see that someone

who has been lucky and paying attention
is just about to go out . . . but honestly
who cares? Someone has to lose,
and why shouldn't that someone be you?

The Small Towns

In the small towns, giant butterflies are clamped
to the sides of houses, and deer stand
in stocking feet on the green lawns.

The wishing wells are all for sale.

Pinwheels of daisy wood are turning in the wind.
In the small towns, the feed mills scrape
the sky with silver fingers, fat cars park
in slanting rows on Main Street.

In the small town cafes, flies buzz against the glass
in the pie case, the coffee is weak, and
the plastic menus are stuck behind the
napkin holders. The waitresses

in the small towns are about to go off to college
where they will read Henry James
and James Joyce. They will sit down to
white linen and crystal.

Soon they won't be happy anywhere.

The Other Farm

I noticed that things were different there:
the kitchen, with its one bare bulb, the slop
pail under the cracked sink, the oil cloth on
the table. Upstairs, the rooms were freezing

and bare, so we played in a corner of
the kitchen, or (mostly) we went outside
to the haybarn and played with the kittens
(there were always kittens): gray ones, soft as

charcoal, tiger-striped ones, and calicos,
like something out of that Wanda Gag book
with the millions of cats, which was just what
I wanted back then — and that's why I thought

we were the poor ones, since we only had
a cat named Fluffy and a dog named Spot.

Country Roads

It was one of those days
when the sun poured gold
into the air, and flecks of
light floated in shafts that
fell through the branches
of yellow leaf and green.

We'd had dinner at a place
on the edge of a lake, and
now we were going back
to town. There was a simple
way to get there, but she
didn't take it. Instead, we

drove the country roads
with the corn rows flicking by,
each one visible for a half
second, then gone. "Hello,
hello, hello," they said, then
"Good-bye, bye, bye, bye."

The soybeans, we agreed,
had turned burgundy overnight,
but it was the cornfields we
watched, as if we were waiting
for the waters to open, as if
we might cross over Jordan.

Back Before

> *There is a house that is no more a house*
> *Upon a farm that is no more a farm*
> *And in a town that is no more a town.*
> — Robert Frost

This was when the house was still a house,
and the farm was everything a farm
was meant to be; this was before the town
swallowed up the fields with streets and houses.

We lived on that farm, never dreaming that
anything about it would ever change —
it seemed immortal to us, poor mortals,
as if our loving it would make it last.

About wind and fire we knew that either
would suffice to end our world, but there were
years when the apple trees were filled with fruit
and the grapes hung heavy on the vine.

We were climbers of ladders and birches —
what did we know of the ruins of time?

The Last Perfect Season

No one knew it then, but that was the last
perfect season, the last time sky and earth

were so balanced that when we walked,
we flew, the last time we could pick a crate

of strawberries every morning in June,
the last time the mystical threshing

machine appeared at the edge of the field,
dividing the oats from the chaff, time of

hollyhocks and sprinklers, white clouds over
a tin roof. Everyone we knew was young then.

Our mothers wore dresses the color of
dove wings, slim at the waist, skirts flaring

just enough to let the folds drape slightly,
like the elegant suits our fathers wore,

shirts so white they dazzled even
the grainy eye of the camera when

we looked down into the viewfinder to
press the button that would keep us there,

as if we already knew that this was
as good as it was ever going to get.

Acknowledgments

"Uncle Al and Uncle Floyd Shoot Some Pool," *Whistling Shade*
"Say Uncle," *Dickinson Review*
"Our Fathers," *Seminary Ridge Review*
"The Exam," *American Life in Poetry*
"The Blue in the Distance," *Kean Review*
"Things I Know," *The Writer's Almanac*
"Fairy Tales," "Apple Trees at the Farm," *Green Blade*
"After That," in *From the Other World: Poems in Memory of James Wright*
"Back Before," *Seminary Ridge Review*
"The Piano," *Lascaux Review*
"Grandma Clara," "September Afternoons," *And the Humming* (Chapbook)
"In Winter," *Flurry*

About the Author

Joyce Sutphen grew up on a farm near St. Joseph, Minnesota and currently lives in Chaska, Minnesota. She has degrees from the University of Minnesota, including a Ph.D. in Renaissance Drama. Her first book, *Straight Out of View*, won the Barnard New Women's Poets Prize (Beacon Press, 1995, republished by Holy Cow! Press in 2001). *Coming Back to the Body* (Holy Cow! Press, 2000) was a finalist for a Minnesota Book Award, and *Naming the Stars* (Holy Cow! Press 2004), won a Minnesota Book Award in Poetry. In 2005, Red Dragonfly Press published *Fourteen Sonnets* in a letterpress edition, and in 2006 Sutphen co-edited the award-winning anthology *To Sing Along the Way: Minnesota Women Poets from Pre-Territorial Days to the Present* (New Rivers Press). *House of Possibility*, a letter press edition of poems, was published by Accordion Press in 2012. Her poems have appeared in *Poetry*, *American Poetry Review*, *Atlanta Review*, *Minnesota Monthly*, *North Dakota Review*, and many other journals, and she has been a guest on *A Prairie Home Companion*, hosted by Garrison Keillor. She is the second Minnesota Poet Laureate, succeeding Robert Bly.